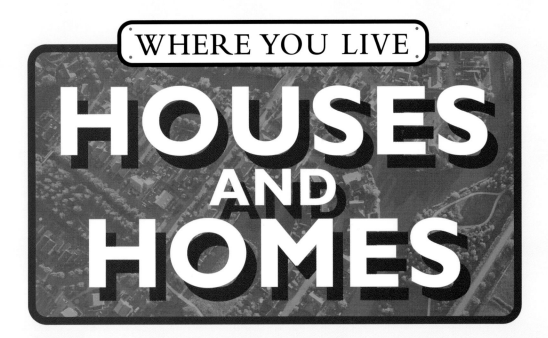

WHERE YOU LIVE

HOUSES AND HOMES

Ruth Nason

Photography by Chris Fairclough

FRANKLIN WATTS
LONDON • SYDNEY

First published in 2007 by
Franklin Watts
338 Euston Road
London NW1 3BH

Franklin Watts Australia
Level 17/207 Kent Street
Sydney NSW 2000

ISBN 978 0 7496 7175 4

Dewey classification number: 728

A CIP catalogue record for this book is available
from the British Library.

Planning and production by Discovery Books Limited
Editor: Paul Humphrey
Designer: Ian Winton
Photography: Chris Fairclough

Printed in China

Franklin Watts is a division of Hachette Children's Books.

Photo acknowledgements
All the photographs in this book were supplied by Chris Fairclough except for the
following: pages 21 E-OnUK/Newscast, 26 (top) David Chambers/Arcaid, 27 Mike
Nason.

Note about questions in this book
The books in the Where You Live series feature lots of questions for readers to answer.
Many of these are open-ended questions to encourage discussion and many have no
single answer. For this reason, no answers to questions are given in the books.

Contents

What is a home?

A home is a place to live. Homes give shelter from the world outside. People like to make their homes comfortable.

People live in many different types of homes.

A home can be grand, like a **palace** or a **castle**.

A home can be a house or a flat.

- Which types of home can you see in the picture on the right?
- Which other types of home can you think of?
- Which types of rooms make up a home?

Even a boat can be a home.

- What would it be like to live on a boat?
- What colour is your front door?
- What things do people need on or by the door to their home?

All homes have a door. Inside is a place to
- stay warm and dry
- rest and sleep
- eat meals and spend time with your family
- keep your belongings.

WHERE YOU LIVE
See which types of homes you spot on a walk around your town or village.

7

Old and new

Some of the oldest houses you will see are more than 400 years old. Over the years, people have repaired and changed these houses in some ways.

- Can you guess how many people might have lived in a house that is 400 years old?
- How is this house different to a modern one?

Houses like the two on this page are called **timber-framed**. Timber means wood. The builders made a frame from wood. They filled in the spaces with **wattle and daub** or with **bricks**.

Tall **chimneys** are sometimes a clue that houses are quite old. Some new houses have no chimneys.

- What are chimneys for?
- Why don't the houses on the left have chimneys?
- Do you think the block of flats below is old or new?

WHERE YOU LIVE
Look for homes that have a date that tells you when they were built. Work out how old they are. Find out whose coronation took place in 1902.

CORONATION
~ COTTAGES ~
— 1902 —

Building materials

At first, builders always used materials from nearby, such as wood, stone, mud and straw. This changed as methods of transport developed.

Today, many homes are built from bricks. The bricks may come from a brickworks far away. Bricks are made from **clay**.

Look for patterns made with bricks. In **Victorian** times, many builders used different-coloured bricks to make patterns.

- How old are houses that were built in Victorian times?
- Which things in this picture did not exist in Victorian times?

Some buildings are made from stone. These flats were built from blocks of **sandstone**.

The stone and brick **cottage** (below) has a **thatched** roof.

- What colour is sandstone?
- What is a thatched roof made from?
- Which other materials are used for roofs?

WHERE YOU LIVE
Look for stone carvings on houses.

11

Different types of houses

Count how many houses you can see on these two pages. The houses are different in several ways.

These houses are joined in a row called a terrace. People have painted their houses different colours.

- Why do these houses have a small roof over the front door?
- Which two houses have window **shutters**?
- How many **storeys** do the houses have?

WHERE YOU LIVE
Look for ways that people have made their house look different from others in your street.

• Why do houses have sloping roofs?

• Which house on these two pages would you like to live in? Why?

• Do all your friends like the same one as you?

This house is not joined to another one. It is called a detached house.

Two houses joined in a pair are called semi-detached houses.

Bungalows and flats

A **bungalow** has all of its rooms on one floor. There are no stairs to climb.

• Why do some people choose a home that has no stairs?
• How many steps and stairs are there in and around your home?

This bungalow has **solar panels** on its roof. They collect energy from the Sun. The energy is used to help heat the water for the people in the bungalow.

A flat is called a flat because all of its rooms are on one floor.

There may be many flats in one tall block. Or a building might contain just two or three flats.

Some flats have a **balcony**.

•How do people reach the flats at the top of a tall block?
•What do people use their balconies for?

WHERE YOU LIVE
Look at the names of blocks of flats. Try to tell why the names were chosen.

15

What's outside?

People like houses with gardens. Gardens are good places to grow flowers or relax in. They are also a safe place for children to play.

The cottages (above) have long front gardens.

This house (right) has no front garden. The front door opens on to the street.

●What problems could there be in a house that opens on to the street?

●What are the walls of this house made from?

These houses were built before people had
cars. Now people keep their cars in the street.

Many new homes are built with places for cars,
such as garages, driveways and parking spaces.

• Where do people keep their cars in your street?

• What problems are there when lots of cars are parked in a street?

17

Windows

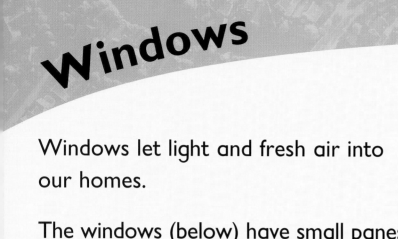

Windows let light and fresh air into our homes.

The windows (below) have small panes of glass called **leaded lights**.

- What shapes are the panes of glass in the windows on the left?
- Why are the windows above the doors of the houses below called **fanlights**?

Windows that stick out from a sloping roof are called dormer windows.

Large windows that open like doors are called patio doors, or French windows.

• How do you open your windows at home?
• Which types of windows do you like best?

A bay window (right) sticks out like a box.

A bow window (below) curves outwards.

You open and close some windows by sliding them up and down (left). They are called sash windows.

WHERE YOU LIVE
Count how many types of windows you can spot around your village or town.

What's inside?

Small flats sometimes only have one or two rooms, but most homes have more than this.

There might be a kitchen to cook in (above). There might also be a dining room to eat in (left).

- How many rooms are there in your home?
- Which is the biggest room?
- Which is the smallest room?
- Which is your favourite room?

A home might have a living room to relax in (above). There will be bedrooms to sleep in (left).

There are lots of services that come into a home. They might include:

- gas
- electricity
- water
- telephone
- cable or satellite television
- oil for central heating.

- What services come into your home?
- What do you call the person who mends water systems?
- How does waste water leave your home?

WHERE YOU LIVE
Draw a plan of all the rooms in your home. Draw on all the furniture and all the kitchen fittings.

Who are homes built for?

Many homes are built so that people can live near their work. Can you guess what type of worker this house was built for?

In Victorian times, people moved from the country to work in towns. Many terraced houses were built for them.

• What examples can you find of homes built for workers?

• Which streets in your town were built in Victorian times?

You may find homes for students or for elderly people. These new flats have been built for **retired** people.

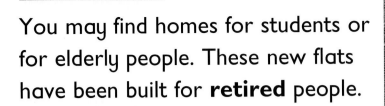

In the past, rich people sometimes gave money to build **almshouses** like these (below) for poor people. The almshouses have a plaque on the wall, which tells you who built them.

- What new homes are being built where you live?
- Who built the almshouses below?
- Who lived there?

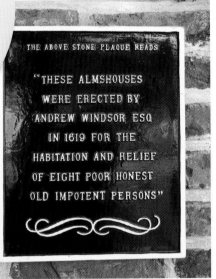

THE ABOVE STONE PLAQUE READS

"THESE ALMSHOUSES WERE ERECTED BY ANDREW WINDSOR ESQ IN 1619 FOR THE HABITATION AND RELIEF OF EIGHT POOR HONEST OLD IMPOTENT PERSONS"

WHERE YOU LIVE
Look for almshouses in your area. Find out about their history.

Changes people make

Look around to see changes that people make to their homes.

One way to change a building is to paint it a different colour.

Some people make changes to **modernise** an old home.

- Which colour would you choose to paint a house?
- How can you tell that these houses have televisions?
- What things do people change in order to modernise a building?

Have you seen people take out windows and put in new ones? Many people choose windows with plastic frames, because plastic does not need to be painted.

Some people need more room and so they build an **extension**.

WHERE YOU LIVE

Look for old buildings, such as churches or workplaces, that have been changed into homes. The picture (right) shows a **warehouse** that has been turned into flats.

- Why might a family need more room in their home?
- Do the black lines painted on the left-hand house below make you think of another house in this book?

79

25

Homes for the future

There are plans to build many new homes in the UK.

Some new homes look modern. Some are made to look like buildings from past times. The new houses below look like smart Victorian homes.

- Do you prefer the look of older or more modern homes?
- What types of windows do the houses above have?

Today we must prevent air **pollution** as much as we can. We should use less electricity, which is made at power stations that pollute the air. In the future all homes could have things that help people to use less electricity.

A **sun pipe** brings lots of sunlight into the house (right).

A wind turbine (above) makes electricity in a clean way.

•How does a sun pipe help people to use less electricity?
•What else is on the roof of this house?
•How can you use less electricity at home?

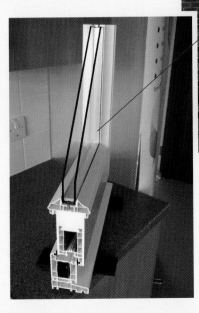

Double-glazed windows (left) stop heat escaping from the house.

WHERE YOU LIVE
Draw and label a picture of the best home you can think of for the future.

27

Glossary

Almshouses Small houses that were built and paid for by a rich person, in order to provide homes for some of the very poorest people in the town or village.

Balcony A platform that sticks out from a building and has a wall or railing around its three edges. People in the building can walk onto the balcony through a window.

Bricks Blocks made from clay. The clay is moulded into shape and then dried or baked.

Bungalow A home with just one storey.

Castle A large house in the country for an important person. At first, castles were built as very strong places, to keep people safe if their enemies attacked.

Chimneys Passageways over fireplaces, leading up to the open air. Smoke and fumes from the fire rise up the chimney, out into the air.

Clay A type of earth.

Cottage A small house, especially in the country.

Double-glazed Made from two layers of glass, with air trapped between them. Windows like this act like a double layer of clothing, keeping warm air inside the house.

Extension A part of a building that is added on later, to make the whole building bigger.

Fanlights Windows in the shape of an open fan, usually found above a door.

Leaded lights Windows with small panes of glass separated by dark metal strips.

Modernise To change an old building so that it becomes as comfortable as a modern one.

Palace A large and splendid house, the home of someone rich and important, such as a king or queen.

Pollution Dirt, waste and poison.

Retired No longer going to work. Many people retire at about the age of 65.

Sandstone A rock made from grains of sand that have been squashed together under the ground.

Shutters Wooden or metal covers that close over a window.

Solar panels Thin layers of a special material that are fixed in a place where they can take in energy from the Sun. This is used to heat water or create electricity.

Storeys Floors in a building.

Sun pipe A long tube with glass at the top. The glass is designed to catch lots of sunlight, which is channelled down the tube into the house below. The sun pipe provides light for the house. The people use less electricity than before, when they always used electric lights.

Thatched Covered with straw, reeds, heather or a natural material like that.

Timber-framed With a frame made from wood.

Victorian To do with Queen Victoria. She was queen of Great Britain from 1837 to 1901.

Warehouse A large hall or building where goods are stored, for example at a factory.

Wattle and daub Materials used for building walls in the past. Wattle is twigs and sticks, woven together. It was then covered or 'daubed' with sticky mud, and this dried to become a strong wall.

Further information

http://www.woodlands-junior.kent.sch.uk/customs/topics/index.htm has useful information for projects about Britain. You can look up a topic, such as Homes, in the long A to Z list.

http://www.ngfl-cymru.org.uk/vtc/where_we_live/eng/Introduction/default.htm has some games to play, to check what you have learnt about houses and homes.

You can see what homes were like in the past at http://www.bbc.co.uk/education/dynamo/history/stepback.htm

You can find out about kitchens in the past and present at http://www.ngfl-cymru.org.uk/vtc/kitchen_past_present/eng/Introduction/default.htm

http://www.buildingconnections.co.uk/ has lots of fun activities for young people at different levels. Click on Activities and start at Level 1.

Older children could try the games about sustainability (including building an environmentally friendly house) at http://www.mysusthouse.org/game.html

For teachers, http://www.architecturecentre.co.uk/education/ has a really useful link to a list of Teaching Resources/Links.

The Museum of Domestic Design and Architecture http://www.moda.mdx.ac.uk/ also has activities for schools. (Follow the link to Educational resources.)

Books

Family Scrapbook: Home Life in the 1950s and 60s, Faye Gardner, 2005 (Evans Publishing)

History Snapshots: Homes, Sarah Ridley, 2007 (Franklin Watts)

I Can Help Save Energy, Viv Smith, 2001 (Franklin Watts)

I Can Help Save Water, Viv Smith, 2001 (Franklin Watts)

Safety First: In the Home, Ruth Thompson, 2004 (Franklin Watts)

Start-Up History: Homes, Stewart Ross, 2003 (Evans Publishing)

Ways Into History: Houses and Homes, Sally Hewitt, 2005 (Franklin Watts)

Why Manners Matter: In the Home, Jillian Powell, 2005 (Franklin Watts)

Index